Polar Bears

Sally Cowan

Contents

What Are Polar Bears?

Polar bears are the largest bears on Earth.
They live in the **Arctic**, near the North Pole.
It is one of the coldest environments on Earth.

Polar bears spend most of their lives **roaming** the sea ice.
This is where they hunt for food.

A polar bear mother and cub roam the sea ice.

Living in the Cold

Polar bears have large, solid bodies with a thick layer of fat. The fat helps them to stay warm.

Their fur is also important for warmth.
Two layers of thick fur cover their skin.

Polar bears are strong swimmers.
They have powerful front legs with large, webbed paws like paddles. Their narrow heads and long necks allow them to move smoothly through the water.

Polar bears use their large paws to swim.

Their thick, sharp claws are for digging into the ice and for grabbing prey. Large teeth and powerful jaws allow polar bears to tear their prey apart.

Sea Ice

The sea ice of the Arctic Ocean is the main **habitat** of polar bears. It is where they hunt seals to eat.

The amount of sea ice changes during the year. In autumn and winter, the ocean freezes for thousands of kilometres. The sky is dark for much of the time as polar bears roam the large areas of ice. The bears walk slowly and steadily over long distances for many hours.

Even in the coldest areas of the Arctic, the sea ice is only a few metres thick.

Polar bears walk long distances on the sea ice.

If there are storms, polar bears dig a hole in the ice or snow for shelter. They curl up inside the hole, out of the wind.

A polar bear comes out of a hole in the snow after a storm.

In the Arctic during spring and summer, there is daylight for almost 24 hours a day. The weather gets warmer and more than half of the sea ice melts.

It is much harder for polar bears to find seals, so the bears must move to the land.

A polar bear moves to the land during the Arctic summer.

A male polar bear searches for food on the land during the Arctic summer.

Hunting and Food

Seals are the favourite food of polar bears. The bears need to eat seal **blubber** to build up their own layer of body fat.

During the colder months, seals make holes in the sea ice. They have to swim up from under the water to breathe. Sometimes, they come out of the holes to rest on the ice.

A seal pokes its head out of a hole in the ice to breathe.

Polar bears can find seal holes using their strong sense of smell. They wait quietly next to a hole for hours, or even days. When a seal comes to the surface, the polar bear can move quickly to grab it.

If a seal is resting on the ice, a polar bear can run surprisingly fast to catch it.

A polar bear waits beside a seal hole.

When the weather is warmer, there is less sea ice. Seals do not need to make breathing holes. They stay out in deep water.

Polar bears cannot swim fast enough to catch seals in the water. The bears must move to the land to **scavenge** food such as dead birds and whales.

Polar bears can eat a huge amount at once. Then, they do not need to eat again for several days.

A scavenging polar bear finds a dead whale to eat.

Sometimes, walruses and small whales swim into shallow water near the shore. Large polar bears can attack and kill them for food.

A large polar bear can catch and eat a walrus.

Polar Bear Cubs

In autumn, female polar bears dig a den in the snow to have their cubs. Falling snow covers the entrance to the den.

Polar bears usually have twin cubs.
The tiny cubs are born blind,
with no teeth and short fur.

Most female polar bears give birth to twin cubs.

The mother stays in the den for the winter to keep the cubs warm and feed them milk. For months, the mother does not eat anything. She gets thinner and hungrier.

When the weather warms up, the mother and cubs break out of the den.

The cubs stay with their mother for about two years.
She teaches them important skills,
such as hunting and swimming.

A mother polar bear teaches her cubs to hunt.

Male polar bears live alone.
In spring, they search for a female to **mate** with.
Sometimes, the males fight over one female.
The male does not stay with the female
or help her with the cubs.

Large males can be dangerous around cubs. When food is hard to find, hungry male polar bears sometimes kill cubs to eat them.

When standing on their hind legs, male polar bears can be up to 2.4 metres tall.

Living Alongside Polar Bears

The Inuit (say: *In-yoo-it*), one of the **Indigenous peoples** of Canada, have lived alongside polar bears for centuries.

The Inuit have always hunted polar bears for their meat and **pelts**. Today, there are strict rules to make sure only a small number of polar bears are hunted each year.

The Inuit only hunt a polar bear when they need food. The meat is shared within the community.

An Inuit man wears clothing made from a polar bear pelt.

Sometimes, polar bears come close to Inuit communities in search of food. The Inuit have special guards who make sure that people and their dogs are safe from hungry polar bears.

A polar bear searches for food near an Inuit community.

Surviving a Warmer Earth

The **climate** of Earth is getting warmer.
It is changing the habitat of polar bears.

Now, there is not as much sea ice covering the Arctic Ocean, even in winter. Polar bears must wait longer each year before they can leave the land and hunt seals.
Hungry polar bears can become very weak.
The females have fewer cubs, and the cubs may not survive.

A hungry polar bear searches for food.

In spring, the sea ice is melting earlier than usual. The ice is also thinner, so it melts quickly. Polar bears can become **stranded** in the sea hundreds of kilometres from land.

A polar bear roams on thin ice.

If the climate keeps getting warmer, life will become more difficult for polar bears. They will have to find other foods, such as birds' eggs and **caribou**. These foods are not as good for polar bears as seal blubber.

It is important to protect polar bears and their habitat so that they can survive into the future.

Glossary

Arctic (*proper noun*)	the area around the North Pole, including sea, ice and land
blubber (*noun*)	a layer of fat under the skin of some mammals that swim
caribou (*noun*)	a type of large deer, also called reindeer
climate (*noun*)	the weather patterns throughout the year
habitat (*noun*)	places where animals usually live
Indigenous peoples (*proper noun*)	the first peoples living in an area
mate (*verb*)	to make babies together
pelts (*noun*)	the skin of animals with the fur attached
roaming (*verb*)	walking or swimming around an area
scavenge (*verb*)	to find dead animals or rubbish
stranded (*adjective*)	left in a place with no way to get away

Index